THE HERITAGE COLLECTION

WINSOME EARLE-SEARS
THE AMERICAN DREAM

Letitia deGraft Okyere

Illustrated by Nouman Zafar

Winsome Earle-Sears: The American Dream

Copyright © 2022 by Letitia deGraft Okyere

Illustrator: Nouman Zafar

Layout designer: Nasim Malik Sarkar

Library of Congress Control Number: 2022906815

All rights reserved.

No part of this publication may be reproduced, stored in a retrieval system, a database, and/or published in any form or by any means, electronic, mechanical, photocopying, recording or otherwise, without the prior written permission of the publisher.

ISBN 978-1-956776-05-8 hardback
ISBN 978-1-956776-06-5 ebook

Published by Lion's Historian Press
https://www.lionshistorian.net/

*In memory of
DeJon, Victoria, and Faith*

Excerpt from Winsome Sears' victory speech in November 2021

> I'm here because you voted for me.
>
> I'm here because you put your trust in me.
>
> I'm telling you, what you are looking at, is the American Dream!

CONTENTS

Chapter 1: The November 2021 Victory 1

Chapter 2: Born in Jamaica 3

Chapter 3: U.S. Marine Corps 5

Chapter 4: Family Life 7

Chapter 5: Early Years in Service to Community 9

Chapter 6: The Virginia House of Delegates 11

Chapter 7: Other Community Experience 13

Chapter 8: 2004 Contest for the U.S. Congress 15

Chapter 9: Life in Winchester 17

Chapter 10: A Family Tragedy 19

Chapter 11: 2018 Contest for the U.S. Congress 21

Chapter 12: November 2021 Elections 23

Chapter 13: A Brief Reflection 25

Glossary 27

Quiz 29

References 30

Fun Fact About the Commonwealth of Virginia 32

Other Books in the Heritage Collection 33

Chapter 1
The November 2021 Victory

On November 2, 2021, Winsome Sears, as the Republican Party candidate, defeated her opponent by fifty thousand votes. She became the first woman and first woman of color to be elected to office in the state of Virginia, or the Commonwealth of Virginia.

Winsome was the unlikely candidate, with the odds stacked against her victory. She was one of thirteen candidates, five Republicans and eight Democrats, who contested for the lieutenant governor position. However, Winsome persevered and made history, inaugurated by Virginian officials on January 15, 2022, as the 42nd lieutenant governor.

The story of Winsome Sears's life is one of inspiration and dedication. Her goal in life is to bring light to any given situation rather than revel in darkness. As she explained, to carry light is to seek solutions to problems. To stay in the darkness is to remain a victim. Winsome Sears thus decided to live a life motivated by her desire to change her world, meaning this 2021 victory did not happen by accident. Read about Lieutenant Governor Winsome Earle-Sears and how she broke glass ceilings.

Chapter 2

Born in Jamaica

Winsome was born in Kingston, Jamaica, in 1964. At an early age, her parents noticed she was eager to help her neighbors and was concerned when people in her neighborhood suffered hardship. She lived in a vibrant community and saw what difference a little kindness made to other lives.

Soon, her father decided to seek better life opportunities and moved to the United States in the 1960s with only $1.75 in his pocket. Her father took any job he could find and put himself through school, understanding the value of a good education. Naturally, he sent money home to Jamaica to provide for his family. In those days, the Jamaican currency was stronger than the U.S. dollar, and Winsome's mother would just put the money in the bank.

When Winsome was six years old, her father sent for her to join him in the United States. She arrived at John F. Kennedy Airport in New York in 1970, ready to follow in her father's footsteps, undeterred by her immigrant status. Winsome lived with her family in Bronx, New York, having to adapt to the fast pace of this vibrant city.

Chapter 3

U.S. Marine Corps

After Winsome completed Adlai Stevenson High School with honors, she joined the United States Marine Corps. She was then still a Jamaican citizen, but the country which she adopted as her home had made a significant impact on her life. She believed that it was her turn to give back. Also, the disciplined life of a U.S. Marine would prepare her for life's journey.

She attended the Marine Corps Engineer School, qualifying as a Journeyman Electrician and serving for close to four years as an electrician and diesel mechanic. When she left the Marines in 1986, she had risen to the rank of corporal.

Chapter 4
FAMILY LIFE

Around 1985, Winsome met her husband Terence, and they moved to Norfolk, Virginia. Winsome and Terence built a family of three daughters, DeJon, Katia, and Janel, based on tenets of her Christian faith. She maintained an interest in her children's education, serving as vice president of a parent-teacher association. In addition, they each developed their careers. Terence was a fellow Marine and mechanic.

After the family settled in Norfolk, Winsome enrolled at Tidewater Community College, earning an Associate of Arts degree in 1992. She moved to Old Dominion University, also in Norfolk, graduating with a Bachelor of Arts in English and a minor in Economics. Ten years later, she earned a Master of Arts in Organizational Leadership from Regent University, thinking her future lay in helping other candidates launch effective political campaigns and careers. However, destiny would have other plans for Winsome.

Chapter 5

Early Years in Service to Community

While she worked on her education, Winsome participated in community activities, demonstrating courage and strength of character. She joined the *Volunteers in Service to America* (VISTA), teaching adults to read. She participated in community discussions on educational improvements and religious freedom. Winsome became the regional education manager for the Hampton Roads Chamber of Commerce, helping local businesses to succeed.

She gained experience in politics by working in U.S. Representative J. Randy Forbes's office. Winsome also worked as the director of a women's homeless shelter for the Salvation Army. There, she learned important lessons about effective strategies for helping those in need. Winsome noted that she got her greatest satisfaction when she led a men's prison ministry, teaching troubled men the possibilities of a changed life.

During this time, she had always considered herself a Democrat and voted that way. However, it began to dawn on her that her political values aligned more with the Republican Party during the 1988 presidential campaigns. Then, Winsome heard Republican President George H. Bush say that if all you have is welfare, your children will not receive an inheritance from you. These words stuck with her and threw her into shock, worried about how she would tell her family she had switched sides. She accepted the challenge, being the only Republican in an extended family of Democrats.

Chapter 6

THE VIRGINIA HOUSE OF DELEGATES

Winsome's formal political career began when she was elected by her district to the Virginia House of Delegates in November 2001. This House and the Virginia State Senate, form the Virginia General Assembly as the legislative part of state government.

At the time, Winsome lived in Norfolk, Virginia, and chose to represent her district, which had a large African American population and a long history of voting Democrat. Thus, when Winsome ran for the Virginia House of Delegates, she faced a thirty-one-year established voting pattern. Her opponent, William P. Robinson Jr., had been a delegate for twenty years and his father for ten years prior. Even members of her husband's family campaigned against her. Nonetheless, Winsome won the elections with fifty-three percent of the vote. The district had not voted for a Black Republican since 1865.

Winsome became the first naturalized citizen and the first veteran to serve in the Virginia House of Delegates. During her two-year term at the House from 2002 to 2004, she pushed a bill that would ban cross-burning in the state, aimed at preventing intimidating activities by hate groups. Winsome brought reform to medical and funeral boards, eliminating harmful practices. She also worked on legislation to support parental school choice.

Chapter 7

Other Community Experience

Winsome got involved with the Louisa Swain Foundation based in Wyoming. Louisa Swain was the first woman in the United States of America to vote, on September 6, 1870, in Wyoming, after laws granted women equal political rights as men. Winsome served on the Foundation's Board for years. She assisted in educational efforts for justice, freedom, and democracy. Winsome did not just focus on Virginia; she was willing to lend her expertise across states when called upon.

Chapter 8

2004 Contest for the U.S. Congress

In 2003, after a busy term in the House of Delegates, Winsome decided not to seek reelection. Her daughters were in high school, and she wanted to focus on her family. However, Republican leaders asked that she consider a 2004 contest for the U.S. Congress. After seven months of consideration, she decided to take on this new task.

Winsome entered the race for the U.S. Congress as Representative for Virginia's Third Congressional District. Winsome's opponent, Representative Bobby Scott, had held the seat for eleven years. She lost to him by sixty-nine to thirty-one percent of the votes. She explained that the defeat made her fearless. After learning to cope with the political loss, she became bold in messages that she conveyed. "You realize, just be real. Don't be handled."

Winsome decided to stick to her original plan to focus on her family. She moved to Winchester when her husband was transferred there.

Chapter 9

Life in Winchester

In Winchester, Winsome became the chief executive officer of the Blue Ridge Association of Realtors. She fought to keep the real estate industry and homeowners' associations thriving. Winsome received appointments from the G.W. Bush Administration to the U.S. Census Bureau and the Department of Veterans Affairs Advisory Committee on Women Veterans. Later in 2011, the governor of Virginia appointed Winsome to the Virginia State Board of Education, and members elected her vice president of the Board.

Through all these public appointments, Winsome demonstrated concern for community well-being. Her focus remained on how to improve the living standards and educational opportunities of her constituents.

Later, Winsome and her husband established a plumbing, electrical, and appliance repair business. The business provides household goods repair and maintenance, ranging from upholstery rehabilitation to appliance repair.

Chapter 10

A Family Tragedy

Tragedy struck the family when Winsome's eldest daughter, DeJon, and her granddaughters Victoria and Faith, died from injuries following a vehicular wreck in Northern Virginia one evening in 2012.

Winsome depended on her Christian faith to pull her through this difficult time. Earlier in 2009, Winsome had published, *Stop Being a Christian Wimp!*, a thirty-one-day journey on deepening one's relationship with God. Winsome gained another perspective from this book she had written to help others overcome painful life experiences. She successfully tested the tools she had provided, finding peace after the death of these three close family members.

Chapter 11

2018 CONTEST FOR THE U.S. CONGRESS

After more than a decade away from politics, in 2018, Winsome stood as a Republican write-in candidate for the U.S. Senate, competing against the Republican nominee, Corey Stewart. Winsome knew that write-in candidates never win U.S. Senate races, but she was willing to take on the contest. She pointed out, "Winning is not just in numbers, but it's in doing what is right." Winsome believed that she could represent the interests of her Virginian constituents more effectively.

Though Winsome failed to secure the U.S. Senate seat, she chose to attract more Black voters to the Republican Party and in 2019, assumed the role of national chair of the *Black Americans to Re-elect the President*. Winsome's strategies included drawing Asian, Latino, and other minorities into voting for Republican candidates by touting values these groups identify with. Even though the Republican presidential nominee, Donald Trump, lost the election, polls taken show that more Black people voted in 2020 for the Republican Party than in 2016.

Chapter 12

November 2021 Elections

In 2021, Winsome decided to run for state office. Within the Republican Party, Sears faced five candidates at the Republican Convention to select a candidate. The Republican Convention took place on May 8, 2021, and on May 11, 2021, Winsome won the Republican Party's nomination for lieutenant governor. Her name was listed fifth on the ballot sheet, and she endured five rounds of voting to emerge as the winner.

During the Virginia lieutenant governor race in 2021, again, Winsome was disadvantaged. Her opponent had a more experienced campaign team and more funding. Nevertheless, Winsome emerged with more votes, a victory she called a "God thing." She campaigned on the grounds of protecting the sanctity of life and parental school choice, giving families in low-income neighborhoods better educational opportunities. She had learned to use the authority given to her well, to lead by example, and to stay focused on the concerns of those she represented.

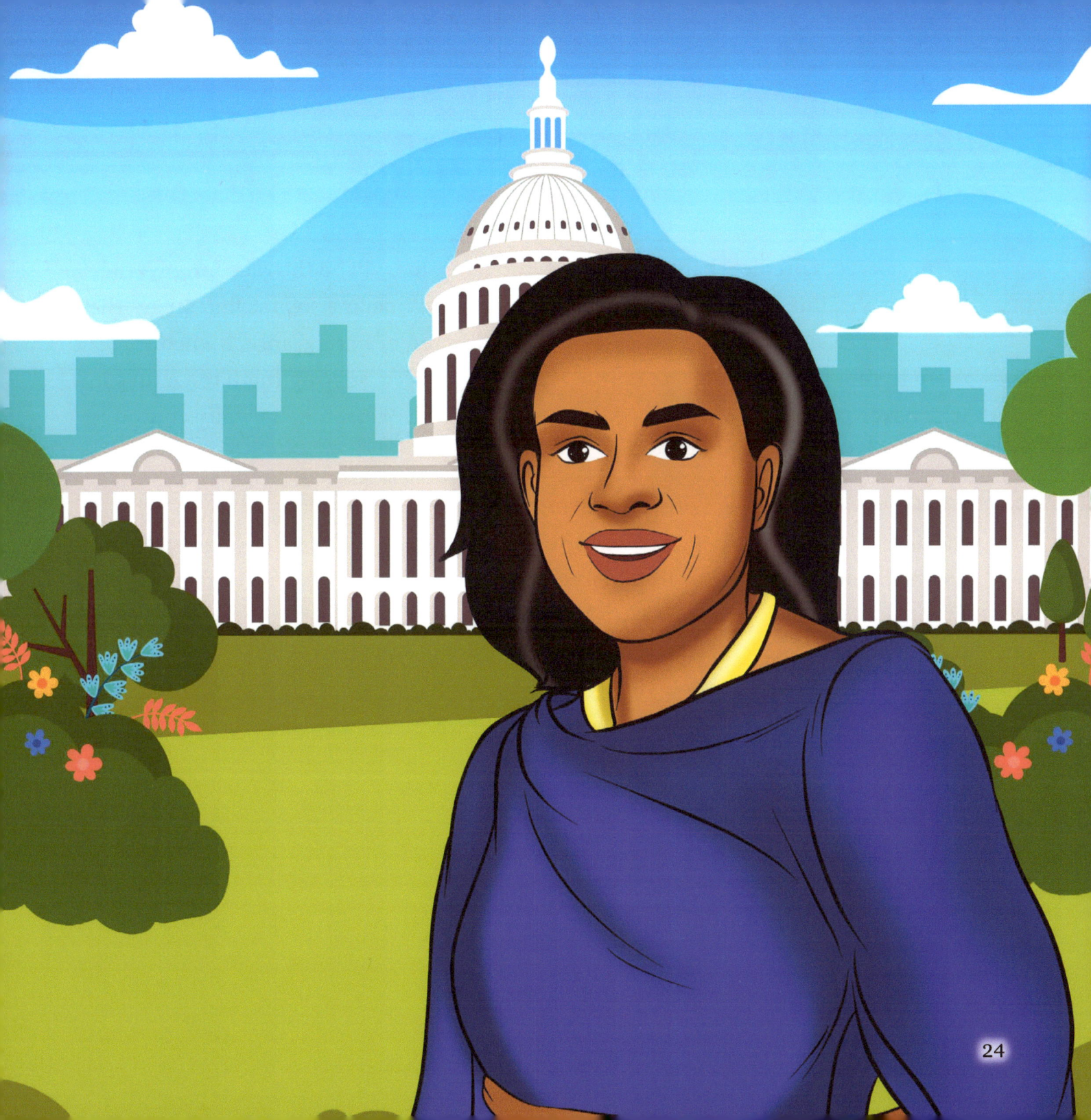

Chapter 13

A Brief Reflection

Observers predict that the next stop for Winsome will be the race for governor of Virginia. Whatever the future holds for Winsome Sears, her story, the American dream, speaks especially to children of immigrants. It encourages them to find their place in the United States of America, stirring them to victory in whichever path taken. Not to be forgotten is that for Winsome, her faith in God is the foundation of all her endeavors.

Winsome's story is also one of redemption. Despite Virginia's history of harsh racial inequality, the state rose from these negative experiences to have the first emancipator, Robert Carter II, who freed five hundred Black slaves. Virginia was the first to elect a Black governor. With Winsome, Virginia elected a naturalized citizen to state office. Over time, these changes demonstrate the potential for righting the wrongs of the past. The problems do not disappear overnight, but the future holds the opportunity for growth and rejection of old ways.

GLOSSARY

Virginia	Commonly known as the Commonwealth of Virginia. It is a state in the southeast region of the United States of America. It has a coastline along the Atlantic Ocean.
Republican Party	The Republican Party is one of the two main political parties in the United States of America. It is also known as the GOP (Grand Old Party) and was founded in 1854.
Democratic Party	The Democratic Party is the other primary political party in the United States of America. It was founded in 1860.
Jamaica	Jamaica is an island country in the Caribbean Sea. Kingston is Jamaica's largest and capital city.
Journeyman Electrician	An electrician is a person who has specialized in placing electrical wires in structures such as buildings and airplanes. A Journeyman Electrician is an electrician who has attained a career step after being an apprentice.
Virginia House of Delegates	The Virginia House of Delegates, with the Virginia State Senate, form the Virginia General Assembly as the legislative part of state government.

Norfolk	Norfolk is a city in the State of Virginia. It is home to the Naval Station Norfolk, the largest naval base in the world.
Naturalization	This is the process by which a person not born in the United States of America becomes a citizen.
The Louisa Swain Foundation	This is a foundation named after the first woman in the U.S.A. to vote, Louisa Swain. The foundation's activities include providing education on freedom, democracy, and human rights.
The Republican Convention	The Republican Convention is the event where members of the Republican Party select the party's representatives for political positions.

QUIZ

1. Where was Winsome Sears born?
   (a) The Bahamas
   (b) Jamaica
   (c) Barbados
   (d) Cuba

2. Which branch of the United States Armed Forces did Winsome join after graduating from high school?
   (a) Marine Corps
   (b) Navy
   (c) Air Force
   (d) Space Force

3. Where did Winsome serve in her first political role?
   (a) U.S. Senate
   (b) U.S. House of Representatives
   (c) Virginia State Senate
   (d) Virginia House of Delegates

4. In which year did Winsome Sears become the Lieutenant Governor of Virginia?
   (a) 2014
   (b) 2016
   (c) 2022
   (d) 2020

Quiz Answers: BADC

REFERENCES

Hunkins, Ray. "Ray Hunkins: Winsome Sears in Wyoming." *Cowboys State Daily*, 22 November 2021, https://cowboystatedaily.com/201/11/22/ray-hunkins-winsome-sears-in-wyoming/. Accessed 12 December 2021.

Nelson, Dean. "Winsome Sears is a trailblazer." *World News Group*, 9 December 2021, https://wng.org/opinions/winsome-sears-is-a-trailblazer-1639050562. Accessed 12 December 2021.

Picket, Kerry. "The return of Winsome Sears." *Washington Examiner*, 10 June 2021, https://www.washingtonexaminer.com/news/the-return-of-winsome-sears. Accessed 13 December 2021.

Hall, Matthew. "Lieutenant Governor Candidate Winsome Sears makes stop in Roanoke." *The Tennessee Star*, 6 May 2021, https://tennesseestar.com/2021/05/06/gop-lieutenant-governor-candidate-winsome-sears-makes-stop-in-roanoke/. Accessed 12 December 2021.

Wilson, Patrick. "Former GOP state delegate wants Republicans to write in her name for US Senate instead of voting for Corey Stewart." *Richmond Times Dispatch*, 18 September 2018, https://richmond.com/news/local/government-politics/former-gop-state-delegate-wants-republicans-to-write-in-her-name-for-u-s-senate/article_65023362-46c2-5d2e-97ba-71eaa0b8a2cb.html. Accessed 13 December 2021.

Germanotta, Tony. "Whatever happened to... that fast-rising black Republican?" *The Virginian-Pilot*, 18 December 2006, https://www.pilotonline.com/news/article_db-0f01c7-fd33-58a7-a64e-c35f3ac86a73.html. Accessed 29 December 2021.

Sizemore, Bill. "Ex-local delegate loses three relatives in fatal wreck." *The Virginian-Pilot*, 8 June 2012, https://www.pilotonline.com/news/article_a8b34e56-61b7-52ca-8a56-d96beb42c52d.html. Accessed 13 December 2021.

"With victory, Sears broke down barriers." *Washington Times*, 23 November 2001, https://www.washingtontimes.com/news/2001/nov/23/20011123-031339-3266r/. Accessed 14 December 2021.

FUN FACT ABOUT THE COMMONWEALTH OF VIRGINIA

The first bank ran by a woman was established in Virginia's capital city of Richmond. Maggie Lena Walker, of African American descent, opened the St. Luke Penny Savings Bank in 1903. She later became the Bank's first president and chairman of the Board of Directors, helping members of the African American community with business activities.

THE COMMONWEALTH OF VIRGINIA

OTHER BOOKS IN THE HERITAGE COLLECTION

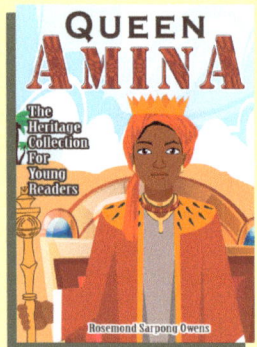
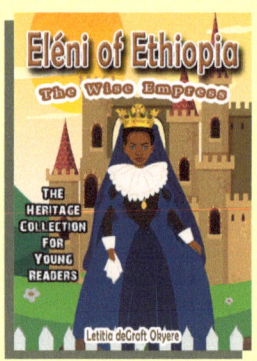

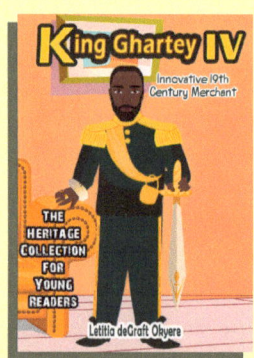
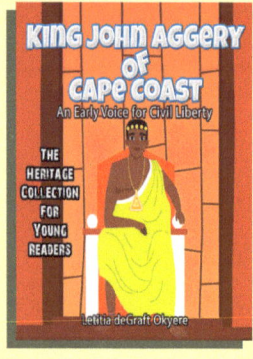

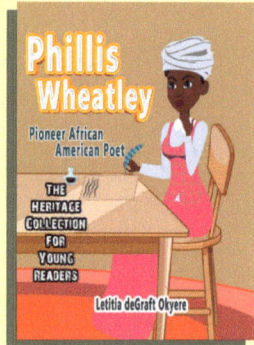
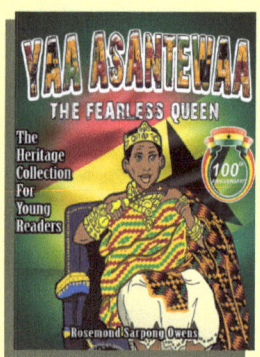

www.ingramcontent.com/pod-product-compliance
Lightning Source LLC
Chambersburg PA
CBHW040757240426
43673CB00014B/375